D0938760

Doorways
of Cape May

918

Tina Skinner
Melissa Cardona

Schiffer Publishing Ltd

4880 Lower Valley Road, Atglen, PA 19310 USA

Copyright © 2005 by Schiffer Publishing, Ltd.
Library of Congress Control Number: 2004112298

Designed by Ellen J. Taltoan
Type set in Zapf Chancery Bd BT/Humanist 521 BT

ISBN: 0-7643-2161-7
Printed in China

Published by Schiffer Publishing Ltd.
4880 Lower Valley Road
Atglen, PA 19310
Phone: (610) 593-1777; Fax: (610) 593-2002
E-mail: Info@schifferbooks.com

For the largest selection of fine reference books on this and related subjects, please visit our web site at **www.schifferbooks.com**
We are always looking for people to write books on new and related subjects. If you have an idea for a book please contact us at the above address.

This book may be purchased from the publisher.
Include $3.95 for shipping.
Please try your bookstore first.
You may write for a free catalog.

In Europe, Schiffer books are distributed by
Bushwood Books
6 Marksbury Ave.
Kew Gardens
Surrey TW9 4JF England
Phone: 44 (0) 20 8392-8585;
Fax: 44 (0) 20 8392-9876
E-mail: info@bushwoodbooks.co.uk
Free postage in the U.K., Europe; air mail at cost.

Introduction

People can't help but fall in love with Cape May. With all its charm, this picturesque town attracts thousands of visitors each year, and keeps them coming back again and again. Listed on the National Register of Historic Places, Cape May beckons tourists with its rich collection of Victorian architecture – fanciful structures bejeweled in bright colors, wrapping verandas, and gingerbread trim – and the opportunity to visit another time in history, when the pace of life was not so hectic, when the world did not seem so complex.

One of the joys of Cape May is strolling along its quaint streets and avenues. Each block offers passersby a unique experience, filled with colorful flower gardens, cozy porches, and enchanting structures. After a week spent wandering through Cape May and exploring the town's delightful side streets and highly trafficked areas, we found much to photograph. What grabbed our attention most, however, were the doorways.

Each with a personality all its own, the portals of Cape May offer a miniature glimpse into what makes the town as a whole so appealing. If the eyes are the windows to a person's soul, then the portals of a town's structures reveal nature of that place and the people that inhabit it. Cape May residents love their homes and their town, and visitors are attracted to that as much as they are to the town's Victorian charm. We saw arched doors with porthole windows, landscaped paths leading up to pretty porches, glass-paned doors hung with lace curtains, and beautiful wooden screen doors, masterfully embellished with scrollwork and coats of paint or finish.

In this book you'll find the doorways of historic homes, mid-century cottages, and newer structures. By no means is it a complete collection of Cape May's eye-catching portals; rather, it's an invitation to meander along the town's peaceful lanes and discover what other hidden treasures lie waiting to be found. Welcome, and enjoy!